To Donna
We ♡ Lori
mahjongg
4eva
♡ Arlene

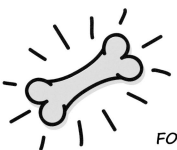

FOR HAROLD YACKER –
The best dad always and forever.

FOR LANCE –
I got lucky at 23, I couldn't ask for a better husband.
Your big heart always has room for MANY more.

FOR JUSTIN AND DYLAN –
You make my life better in every way,
except when I ask you to pick up Marshall's poop.

FOR BARBARA AND MY FAMILY AND FRIENDS –
Thank you for cheering me on!

www.mascotbooks.com

Room for One More

©2018 Arlene Steinberg. All Rights Reserved. No part of this publication
may be reproduced, stored in a retrieval system or transmitted in any
form by any means electronic, mechanical, or photocopying, recording or
otherwise without the permission of the author.

For more information, please contact:
Mascot Books
620 Herndon Parkway, Suite 320
Herndon, VA 20170
info@mascotbooks.com

Library of Congress Control Number: 2018902920

CPSIA Code: PRT0518A
ISBN-13: 978-1-68401-656-3

Printed in the United States

ROOM FOR ONE MORE

Written by ARLENE STEINBERG Illustrated by ALEJANDRO ESCHAVEZ

Marshall and Dewey were
the closest of friends.

Morning till nightfall,
their fun never ends.

They woke up the neighbors and sang to the sun

and always went out for their mid-morning run.

Marshall and Dewey loved to play in the park,
sharing a ball until it got dark.

One day, Ozzie the Portuguese Water Dog came by and greeted Marshall and Dewey with a very shy "Hi."

Ozzie walked away, dejected and sad,
but Marshall and Dewey didn't care, in fact, they were glad!

They whispered,
"Why would we want to make room for one more?
We like each other and that's enough for sure!"

"Making room for one more could mean such work."
"Seriously, what if Ozzie is a **jerk?!**"

"He might bring his toys and
then expect us to share."
"There's <u>no way</u> on Earth that would be fair."

They decided
making room for one more
would be a drag,
until they realized they
needed one more for a game of tag.

HMMMM...Marshall and Dewey
started to think.
What IF making room for one
more actually didn't stink?

So the very next day after singing to the sun and their usual quick mid-morning run,

Marshall and Dewey ran to the park
where this time, Ozzie didn't greet them with a bark.

Marshall and Dewey cried,
"Ozzie, come play, come play with us quick!
Look what we have. It's a brand new stick!"

Ozzie's face lit up with a
GREAT BIG SMILE

that any dog could see for a **mile**.

Together the three played tag all day,
Ozzie jumping right into the fray.

Then frolicking around and learning new tricks.
Adding one more was a really great mix!

Marshall and Dewey learned when you open your heart and mind, you never know what new friends you may find.

photo credit: D. Steinberg

ABOUT THE AUTHOR

ARLENE Y. STEINBERG has been writing stories since she could hold a pencil. She loves taking her chocolate Labrador, Marshall, for walks, but he thinks that he is actually walking her. Arlene lives on Long Island, not only with Marshall, but with her amazing and wonderful husband and sons.